Mel Bay's
Blues Drums Play-Along

Play-Along Tracks for Developing your Blues Drumming Pe

By Kevin Coggins & David Barrett

School of the Blues Lesson Series

CD contents

1	Travelin' Man Blues (E)	17	Travelin' Man Blues Playing Example
2	Muddy's Shuffle (G)	18	Muddy's Shuffle Playing Example
3	In The Box (G)	19	In The Box Playing Example
4	Mr. Green (Fm)	20	Mr. Green Playing Example
5	Major Problem (G)	21	Major Problem Playing Example
6	Minor Problem (Cm)	22	Minor Problem Playing Example
7	Charlie's Swing (Bb)	23	Charlie's Swing Playing Example
8	Uptown Jump (F)	24	Uptown Jump Playing Example
9	The Stroll (F)	25	The Stroll Playing Example
10	The Key (G)	26	The Key Playing Example
11	Good Mojo (E)	27	Good Mojo Playing Example
12	Mr. Rhumba (A)	28	Mr. Rhumba Playing Example
13	Boogie (A)	29	Boogie Playing Example
14	The Tramp (C)	30	The Tramp Playing Example
15	Little Bit (D)	31	Little Bit Playing Example
16	Welcome		

1 2 3 4 5 6 7 8 9 0

Visit us on the Web at www.melbay.com — E-mail us at email@melbay.com

Table of Contents

About This Book & Notation

Many years ago, when I first delved into the recordings of Albert King, James Cotton and Pinetop Perkins, the thought of working with them in their bands was far away, if even a dream for me. I grew up in a sprawling suburb far from the urban rhythm of Chicago and the mystery of the Delta region of the South. It was intimidating for me when I first went to see the blues legends playing in San Jose, California, and hear them play what I was trying to copy from their recordings. Experiencing the music live was an education in itself. After many years of playing with local and regional blues bands I began to work with some of the men who made the music on those records, and they passed along insights and ideas to me of how they wanted the songs to sound and feel. That seems to be the way these traditions are carried on, from one player to another, wanting the song to be familiar, hoping to please the boss.

This book is offered to the student who wishes to learn to play in the style of traditional blues. All of the songs are performed the way we learned to play them, with respect for the sound and feel, and always with an ear for the appropriate style. The bandleader might not know how to call off a Backward Shuffle or a Lump; or a Jimmy Reed beat or a Kansas City Swing. That's why he hired you, hoping that when he or she starts playing, *you* will give the groove what it needs. So listen to lots of recordings in the styles you want to play and study this material. Get down deep into the pocket and let the band relax around what you confidently play.

The jam tracks contained on the accompanying recording represent the most common, or what you can consider "must-know" grooves for a blues drummer. The examples presented for each song are the recommended associated drumming patterns. I have bracketed the main pattern used for each song in the notation. Other than the bracketed main pattern, I play fairly loose, with fills and slight variations throughout to show you the myriad of options available to you within a particular groove. I have tried to convey the importance of playing in the same style as your band mates on each song that you accompany—this is of paramount importance.

About the Author

Kevin Coggins is in high demand as a drum instructor, performer and producer. Voted "Best Blues Drummer" in the San Francisco Bay area, Kevin's list of performing credits reads like a "who's who" of the blues world—Albert King (with whom he has recorded), James Cotton, Otis Rush, Lowell Fulson, Pinetop Perkins, Robert Lockwood Jr., Elvin Bishop, Charlie Musselwhite, Boz Skaggs, and Steve Freund, to name but a few. Although best known for his work with blues performing credits, Kevin is fluent and has taught in all major styles. He is a frequent guest instructor in schools where he works with both small and large ensembles. Kevin is also an avid vintage drum collector and a well-known drum consultant. His drumming articles have appeared in *Not So Modern Drummer*, *Drums and Drumming* and *Music Referral*. He and his two boys reside in San Jose, California.

Kevin's approach to instruction focuses strongly on musicianship and technique. "*Musicianship* is characterized by an overall sense of playing or doing the right thing at the right time, whether by intuition or learned through instruction, in terms of playing a musical instrument or performing in a music group. I consistently explain and apply the basic fundamental principals of musicianship in private lessons and in the seminars that I teach so the player can perform with confidence and self-assurance. I characterize technique as the skill or command in handling the fundamentals of artistic work. *Technique* is a practical method applied to the particular task of performing the fundamentals on a musical instrument. The skillfulness in the command of fundamentals is deriving from practice and familiarity. In fact, practice greatly improves proficiency."

About the School of the Blues Lesson Series

School of the Blues is a school dedicated to the study of blues and all the styles it influenced. Founded in 2002 by educator David Barrett, the school thrives today as the center of blues education in the San Jose/San Francisco, California Bay Area.

The instructors at the school and this lesson series have on average twenty years teaching and performing experience. All of the instructors were hand picked to teach at the school for their playing skills, knowledge of their instrument and ability to teach all skill levels of private and group instruction. We are all dedicated to our craft and receive huge pleasure playing an active role in our students' musical and personal development as well rounded musicians.

This series is a continuation of this love for the blues and its education. David Barrett is the administrator and co-author of all the books. Many meetings took place with all of the instructors to shape the outline of this lesson series and to make sure that the experience and knowledge of the instructors are contained within each book.

This series is also designed for students of other instruments to play together. If you have friends that play harmonica, guitar, keyboard or bass, tell them about this series so that you can grow together. There's nothing more fun than making music with other people.

We all wish you the best of luck in your studies. For more information about this series or to contact us, please visit www.schooloftheblues.com.

Travelin' Man Blues - CD Track 1 (Examples: Track 17)

Key: E

Groove: Double Shuffle with a backbeat and slightly loose hi-hat sound

Tempo: 108bpm (beats per minute)

Intro: From the V (4 measure intro before the standard twelve bar form starts)

Swing/Shuffle rhythm used

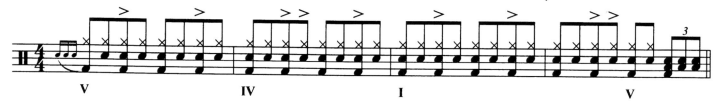

Body: 6 Choruses of standard **12 Bar Blues**

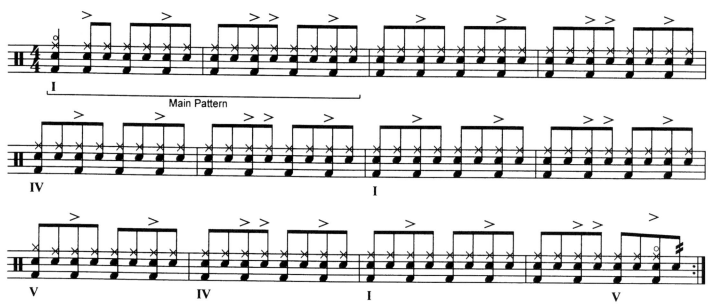

Ending: Band breaks on the downbeat of the 11th measure (I chord). There is a slight ritard at the end (slowing down).

Comments:

In the intro of this song I set up the groove that I will use throughout the song. It is important to remain consistent with the groove from the beginning to the end of the song so its identity remains intact. This is a "double shuffle with a backbeat" (see glossary for a definition of terms). This is a two measure long beat, with an extra accent on the "ah" of beat two in the second measure. A subtle difference from shuffle to shuffle goes a long way in making sure each song stands out from the rest. Note the double stop fill using the floor tom and snare drum at the end of the intro.

Muddy's Shuffle - CD Track 2 (Examples: Track 18)

Key: G

Groove: Double Shuffle with a backbeat and slightly loose hi-hat sound

Tempo: 108bpm

Swing/Shuffle rhythm used
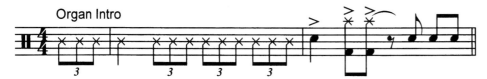

Intro: From the Turnaround (2 measure intro before the standard twelve bar form starts). The keyboard leads in, with the band coming in for two notes before the form begins.

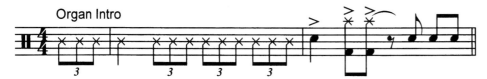

Body: 6 Choruses of standard **12 Bar Blues**. Notice the nice hook played by the guitar and organ.

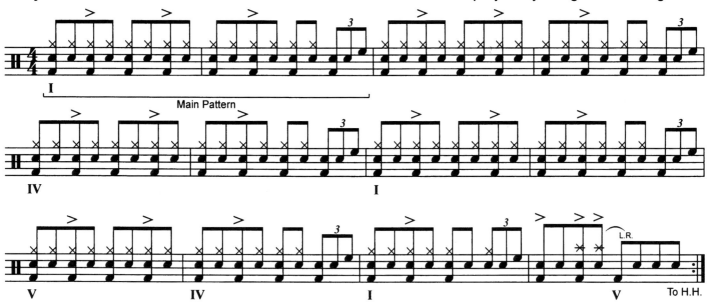

Break: A break is used on the first four measures of the third and sixth choruses.

Ending: Breaks on the 10th measure (IV chord), coming back in on the 11th measure (I chord).

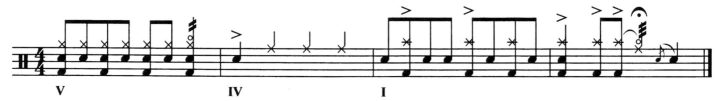

Comments:

After the organ starts this song the drums come in with an accented quarter note. A strong start from the drummer focuses the band's sense of time. This double shuffle pattern is a two-measure long pattern that creates a phrase, which uses a rhythmic device similar to a fill at the end of the phrase that follows the pattern established by the rhythm guitar part. This phrase is repeated throughout the song. The ride pattern can be played on the hi-hat any time you want to introduce a different sound texture (commonly played when backing a vocalist).

In The Box - CD Track 3 (Examples: Track 19)

Key: G

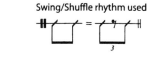

Swing/Shuffle rhythm used

Groove: Double Shuffle with a backbeat

Tempo: 120bpm

Body: 8 Choruses of standard **12 Bar Blues**

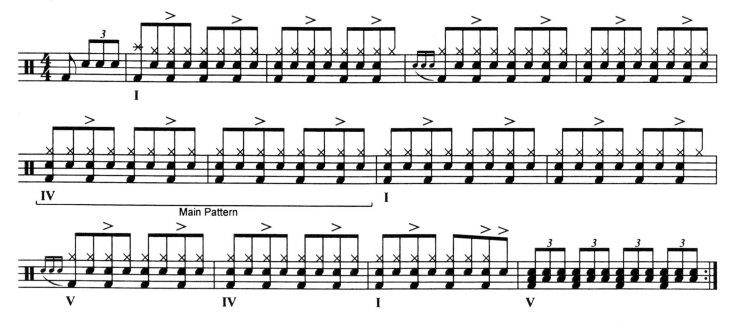

Ending: Band uses standard break on the downbeat of the 11th measure (I chord).

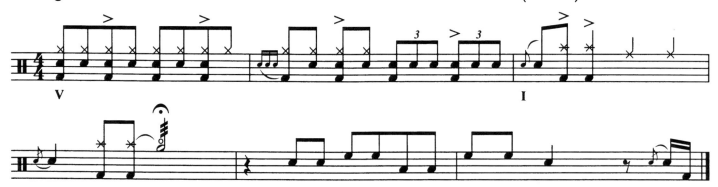

Comments:

Another double shuffle?!? Note the difference from the last two songs. This groove has a simple, consistent, straight-forward shuffle with a driving feel, with drum fills occurring mostly at transition points at the end of each turnaround. Not a lot of extra fills and such here. The style of this groove works because it supports the rhythm section and the soloist without drawing attention away from them. The ride pattern can be played on the hi-hat any time you want to introduce a different sound (commonly played when backing a vocalist).

Mr. Green - CD Track 4 (Examples: Track 20)

Key: F minor

Groove: Green Onions/Help Me

Tempo: 138bpm

Intro: Organ plays for 4 bars, then the band starts on the I (beginning of the form).

Body: 6 Choruses of **12 Bar Blues**.

Ending: At the end of the sixth chorus repeat the last four bars.

Comments:
This particular beat will always identify itself with the classic "Green Onions" groove (Booker T. and the MGs). Note that while the melody is similar to "Help Me," (Sonny Boy Williamson II) the groove is decidedly different. The driving quarter note ride pattern stays on the ride cymbal and the groove remains more forceful without the distraction of doing many drum fills.

Major Problem - CD Track 5 (Examples: Track 21)

Key: G

Groove: Slow Blues with triplet feel

Tempo: 64bpm

Body: 4 Choruses of standard **12 Bar Blues**

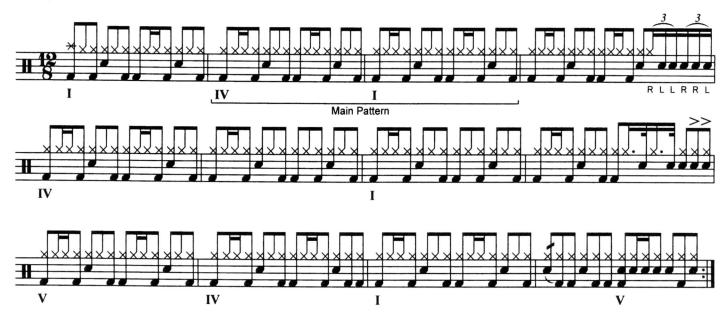

Ending: Band uses standard break on the downbeat of the 11th measure with a stylized line that has a slight ritard at the end.

Comments:
This slow blues has a kind of a jazzy feel, similar to a ballad. Note the added tension in the chord changes that lend to a looser or busier type of drumming style. The tag at the end of the song is a stock ending—easy to follow and straight forward.

Minor Problem - CD Track 6 (Examples: Track 22)

Key: C minor

Groove: Slow Blues with triplet feel

Tempo: 60bpm

Opening: Triplet pickup

Body: 4 Choruses of **12 Bar Blues**. There are many variations that can be used with this triplet feel. The previous song "Major Problem" is one example. For this song I have provided many variations within the first chorus to choose from. Add pickups and fills as you see fit in this type of pattern, just as I have.

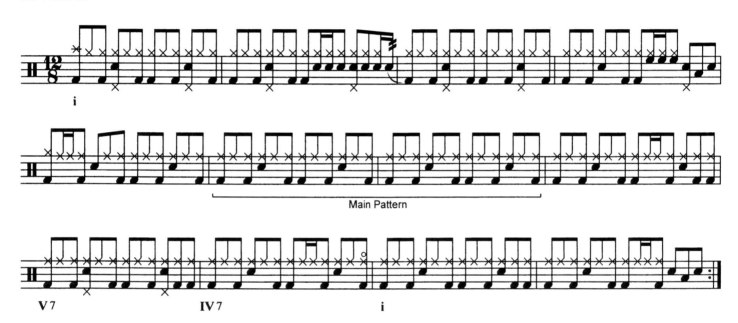

Main Pattern

V 7   IV 7   i

Ending: Band uses standard break on the downbeat of the 11th measure. There is a ritard at the end.

V 7   IV 7   i

Comments:

Here is a typical Chicago style slow blues groove. It has a Muddy Waters feel with lots of double stop fills. When you play a few slow blues songs in a show, it is suggested that each song maintain its own identity. Playing a consistent ride or hi-hat pattern all the way through a song helps to keep it separate from other similar grooves that you will play on the same gig.

Charlie's Swing - CD Track 7 (Examples: Track 23)

Key: B♭

Swing/Shuffle rhythm used

Groove: Uptown Swing with Charleston feel

Tempo: 210bpm

Body: 11 Choruses of **12 Bar Blues** with jazzy changes.

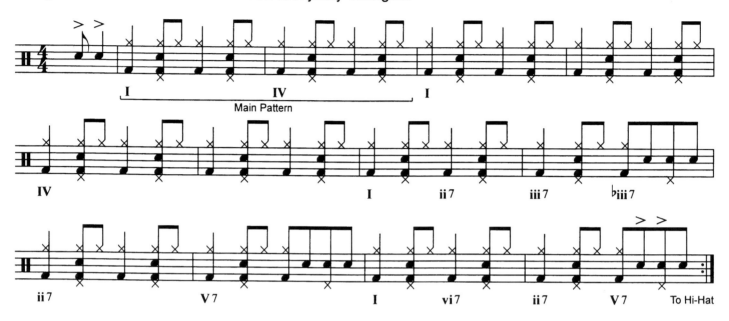

Main Pattern

Ending: The last four measures repeat for a total of three times with slight variation.

Comments:

This song has a swing ride cymbal beat with a strong backbeat to help drive the tempo. I have heard this groove called a "Kansas City Swing." The use of dynamics is especially useful with a repetitive groove like this. Think ahead, if you want to play the "shout chorus" with a strong and driving 2 and 4 on the snare drum, be sure to back off a little in volume on the section just before.

Uptown Jump - CD Track 8 (Examples: Track 24)

Key: F

Groove: Upbeat Jump with backwards shuffle

Swing/Shuffle rhythm used

Tempo: 122bpm

Intro: From the ii (4 measure intro before the standard twelve bar form starts).

Body: 10 Choruses of standard **12 Bar Blues** with no turnaround.

Break: A break is used on the fifth chorus. You can use the line below.

Ending: Band uses standard break on the downbeat of the 11th measure with a unison lick.

Comments:

When the bandleader calls for a backward shuffle and you start playing what is written here, you better hope that this classic beat is what is expected. There is no backbeat on the snare drum when playing a backward shuffle. There is a consistent snare drum stroke on all of the upbeats of the counts of 1—2—3—4. The ride pattern can be played on the hi-hat or ride cymbal and can vary from a quarter note ride pattern, to swing, to shuffle. If the ride pattern is played on the ride cymbal the hi-hat can keep time by playing the 2 and 4 with the pedal. Mix it up to create a unique feel and to create excitement. Remember that this beat is at its best when it lays down a deep pocket for the rest of the band to settle into.

The Stroll - CD Track 9 (Examples: Track 25)

Key: F

Groove: Stroll

Tempo: 108bpm

Swing/Shuffle rhythm used

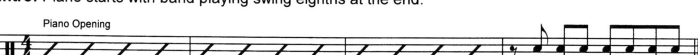

Intro: Piano starts with band playing swing eighths at the end.

Piano Opening

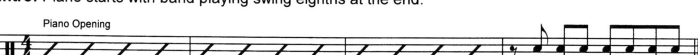

Body: 6 Choruses of an 8 Bar Blues

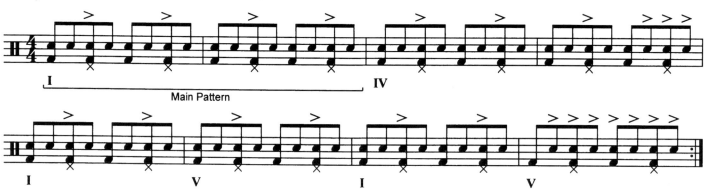

Ending: Band breaks on the downbeat of the 7th measure (common for an 8 bar blues).

Comments:

This groove is accomplished by playing the shuffle pattern on the snare drum with wire or nylon brushes (or something similar) and accenting the backbeats. A light foot plays four beats to the bar on the kick and the 2 and 4 are played on the hi-hat via the foot pedal. The snare drum voices an accented backbeat while keeping a consistent volume on the rest of the pattern. This is a good example of rhythmic phrasing, both in the drum part and with the band as well. The song style calls for a call and response type of phrasing within the melody, with the drummer filling in the holes.

The Key - CD Track 10 (Examples: Track 26)

Key: G

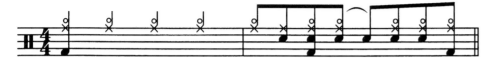
Swing/Shuffle rhythm used

Groove: Shuffle (Jimmy Reed style shuffle on a loosely open hi-hat with a solid backbeat on the snare)

Tempo: 96bpm

Intro: From the Turnaround.

Body: 6 Choruses of an **8 Bar Blues**

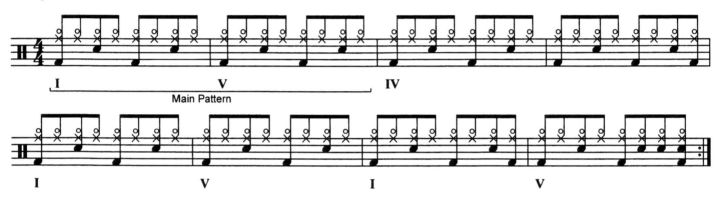

Ending: Band breaks on the downbeat of the 7th measure.

Comments:
Here I play a shuffle ride pattern with a backbeat on the snare drum. My friends from Chicago call this groove a "Lump." It is played in the style of a "Jimmy Reed" song. The hi-hats must maintain a sloshy sound whenever they are played on this type of Jimmy Reed groove. This is not a double shuffle. Notice the lone snare drum hits on the 2 and 4. These hits aren't even rim shots! I loosened the snare wires just a little and then spanked the snare head dead center to get that warm crack that helps define the sound of this style, and also helps to put a different feel to the texture of the groove. Remember this cardinal rule: differentiate each similar groove with some sort of change in sound or style from song to song. If we play every shuffle with the same technique they will all sound the same. It will bore the band, the audience and even you!

Good Mojo - CD Track 11 (Examples: Track 27)

Key: E

Groove: 2 Beat (Country Shuffle)

Tempo: 126bpm is the tempo, though the 2 Beat groove makes it feel twice as fast. For this reason it is sometimes called a cut shuffle.

Intro: From the Turnaround.

Body: 8 Choruses of standard **12 Bar Blues**. Notice the variety of the patterns.

Ending: Band breaks on the downbeat of the 10th measure (IV chord) with the band coming back in on the 11th measure (I chord).

Comments:

The Mojo Beat. Sometimes it is called a "two-beat shuffle." As long as you play in the spirit of the style you can't go wrong. What you play can fall anywhere between simple to complex, but the groove needs to be solid and driving. One of the finest recordings I've heard of this song is the rendition recorded on "Fathers and Sons" (Chess Records), with Muddy Waters on guitar and vocals, Paul Butterfield on harp and Sam Lay on drums. Sam plays a little bit different groove on that recording than what I have played here. Hear how the different grooves are similar while allowing some creative license.

Mr. Rhumba - CD Track 12 (Examples: Track 28)

Key: A

Groove: Rhumba (Rhumba uses straight eights. It doesn't begin as a shuffle or swing rhythm)

Tempo: 126bpm

Intro: From the V.

Body: 8 Choruses of standard **12 Bar Blues**.

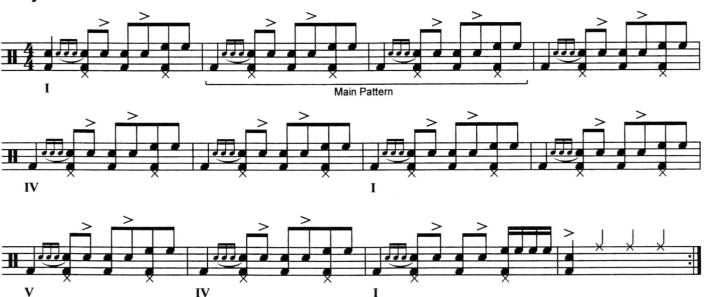

On the 4th and 5th chorus the groove moves to a ***Shuffle***. A standard double shuffle is used here. Detailed below is a sample of what I would play to offer some excitement to this section of the song.

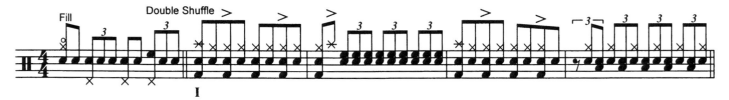

Ending: The band plays the V three times at the end (the last four measures three times) with a "Cha Cha Cha" at the very end.

Comments:
Playing a rhumba is a breath of fresh air amongst the shuffles and slow blues that dominate the landscape of a blues gig, partially due to the license given to move all around the drum set. Here is a chance to play some melodic patterns between the snare drum and toms and to work with the techniques of four-way independence, dynamics and stick control that we drummers work so hard at. Adding to the fun is the contrast created by switching to a shuffle feel and then back to the rhumba. Note the use of double stop fills in the shuffle section and how the fills can be used to add tension to the groove.

Boogie - CD Track 13 (Examples: Track 29)

Key: A

Groove: Boogie (Double Shuffle with a Backbeat)

Tempo: 144bpm

Form: This is a modal blues. Modal means that you stay on the I chord the entire song.

Intro: Guitar plays a 4 bar intro.

Groove Pattern: Double Shuffle on the Ride.

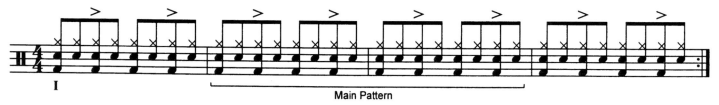

Ending: Band will build for 8 bars and end.

Comments:

This groove is more about attitude than anything else is; it must be relentlessly repetitive and driving in order to work. Keep the intensity up without loosing the feel. Drum fills are the sugar on top, be careful not to over sweeten the taste and destroy the flavor.

The Tramp - CD Track 14 (Examples: Track 30)

Key: C

Groove: Funk Beat

Tempo: 116bpm

Body: 6 Choruses of standard **12 Bar Blues**

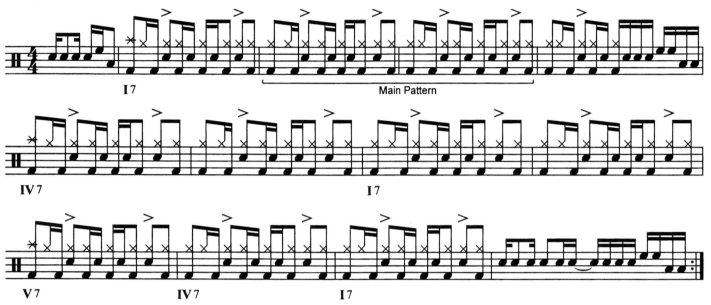

Ending: Band breaks on the downbeat of the 12th measure.

Comments:

This is a funky R&B groove with a strong backbeat. Here you get the chance to "mix it up" with more complex rhythms and fills than what you use in a shuffle. Fill the holes that the rest of the band leaves in the phrases without over-playing and be careful not to step on the soloist or rhythm section.

Little Bit - CD Track 15 (Examples: Track 31)

Key: D

Groove: Rock Beat (Surf Beat or Twist Beat)

Tempo: 168bpm

Body: 4 Choruses of standard **12 Bar Blues**

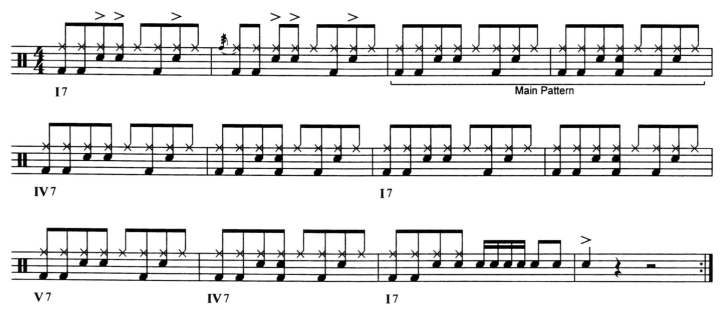

Ending: Band breaks on the downbeat of the 12th measure.

Comments:

The groove here is played because it is in unison with the guitar riff and it also serves up an answer to it as well. Many guitar players will use this riff at least once during a typical gig. This drum groove can also be used as a "Surf Beat," when the bandleader calls off that kind of a thing. Once you start playing the "2 and" snare part you better keep it up through the whole song, or else the song will loose its identity. Remember: choose and lay down a drum pattern at the opening of a song and stick with it so the song retains it's identity, otherwise all of the songs end up sounding alike.

Notation Key

Notation in this book is based on standard drum notation. Shown below are the basic symbols used in drum set notation. Music examples are kept fairly simple to make sure this book is accessible to drummers just above the beginning Level. For best understanding of these techniques reference Mel Bay's *Blues Drums, Level 1* (21066BCD) within this *School of the Blues Lesson Series*.

Drum Set Legend

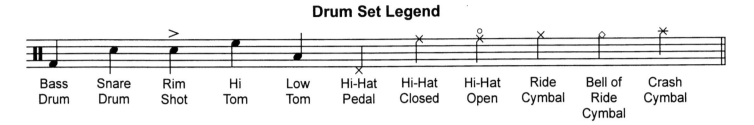

| Bass Drum | Snare Drum | Rim Shot | Hi Tom | Low Tom | Hi-Hat Pedal | Hi-Hat Closed | Hi-Hat Open | Ride Cymbal | Bell of Ride Cymbal | Crash Cymbal |

Glossary of Terms

Accent An emphasis or added volume to a note as compared to the notes next to it. Note the example below from "Travelin' Man Blues." An accent mark is used above beats two and four to show that those beats are to be played stronger (and in this case a rim shot on the snare drum).

Backbeat The backbeat is usually associated with beats two and four in a measure containing four beats. The snare drum is typically used for playing the backbeat. Note the example below from "Travelin' Man Blues." An accent mark is used above beats two and four to show that those beats are to be played stronger, creating the backbeat feel.

Break When the instruments stop playing, before the song has ended, to create a dramatic effect. Note the example below from the ending of "Charlie's Swing."

Build-Up The use of a roll or fill to create a dynamic change of volume.

Call and Response Phrasing Where a short phrase of music is expressed as seeming to offer a question (or call) and then an answer (or response) in the terms of rhythm or melody, that has an easily heard beginning and end, e.g.: "Old MacDonald had a farm, Ee, Ii, Ee, Ii, Oh."

Double Shuffle   When the shuffle pattern is played on two parts of the drum set simultaneously, usually played on the snare drum with either the hi-hat or ride cymbal. Note the example below from "Travelin' Man Blues."

Double-Stop   Where two strokes are used to strike the drums or cymbals, or both, simultaneously. Double-stops are often used to create drum fills in traditional blues drumming. Note the example below from the turnaround of "In The Box."

Dynamics   Degrees of changes in volume.

Fill   Where the drummer stops playing the groove to play one, or a series of notes, usually at the end of a chord progression or to complete a rhythmic phrase. Note the example below from the turnaround of "In The Box."

Lump   A relaxed, medium tempo shuffle with the bass drum playing four beats in each bar and the snare drum playing a strong backbeat on every count of two and four.

Phrase   A short section of a composition into which the music seems naturally to fall. Sometimes a phrase is contained within one breath (for a singer or instrumentalist); sometimes sub-divisions may be used to create the section called a phrase.

Ride Pattern   The consistent playing on the hi-hat, ride cymbal or other instrument of the drum set that provides a consistent pulse of time.

Rhythm   Covers everything pertaining to the *time* aspect of music. This includes the effects of beats, accents or measures; grouping of notes into beats, grouping of beats into measures or grouping of measures into phrases. Rhythm can be played either in a "strict" or "free" sense.

Rhythmic-Phrasing   A phrase made from the components of rhythm, without need of but often using variants of pitch, melody or harmony.

Shuffle   A rhythmic pattern characterized by playing either "swung" eighth notes or dotted eighth and sixteenth notes which are counted as, "One, ah–two, ah–three, ah–four, ah–one..." Note the example below from "The Key."

Swing
A rhythmic pattern characterized by playing either two swing eighth notes or dotted eighth and sixteenth notes which are counted as, "One, two, ah–three, four, ah–one..." Note the example below from "Charlie's Swing."

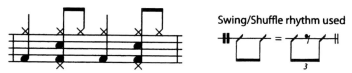

Two-Beat
This beat is usually associated with an up-beat tempo, with the bass drum played on beats one and three and the snare drum being played on beats two and four. Note the example below from "Good Mojo" uses more of a shuffle-style drumming pattern (though not swung), with the addition of sixteenth notes.

School of the Blues Staff
Front Row (L-R): Frank De Rose, John Garcia and Kevin Coggins
Back Row (L-R): Steve Czarnecki and David Barrett

Thanks To...

First and foremost I want to thank David and the rest of the faculty members at School of the Blues for the great work that they did in creating and developing such a tremendous concept. I believe this school is a unique and valuable learning resource for musicians who want to learn how to play this American treasure called The Blues. I also want to express my gratitude to them for having enough faith to bring me aboard as a faculty member so that I could continue to pass along my knowledge and ideas about blues drumming to a captive audience.

I must take this rare opportunity to give thanks in print to some great musicians and bandleaders who took the time and interest to personally help shape my concept as a musician: Christopher Shultis, Steve Freund, Duke Jethro, Francis Clay, Gary Smith, Paul Durkett, Harold Van Winkle, Larry "Arkansas" Davis, C.P. Love, James Cotton, Mitch Woods, Mark Hummel and Larry Cali. Some of these gentlemen were not always congenial with their comments and criticisms, but each one talked to me straight from the heart, and to them I am eternally grateful.

I dedicate this book to my two boys, Michael and Daniel. I hope for them to know that dreams can come true; and that dedication and hard work do produce positive results.

- Producer, Editor & Co-Author – David Barrett
- Musicians – The following musicians performed on the recording.
  - John Garcia (All guitar and vocal work)
  - Frank De Rose (Bass)
  - Kevin Coggins (Drums)
  - Steve Czarnecki (Organ & Piano)
  - Recorded at Soundtek Studios in Campbell, California. Engineered by Thom Duell.
  - Narration recording done at School of the Blues® in San Jose, California.
- Context Proof Readers
  - Dennis Carelli
- Photography – Dave Lepori Photography in San Jose, California